Niels R. Jensen

Maine

Visit us at
www.abdopublishing.com

Published by ABDO Publishing Company, 8000 West 78th Street, Suite 310, Edina, Minnesota 55439 USA. Copyright ©2010 by Abdo Consulting Group, Inc. International copyrights reserved in all countries. No part of this book may be reproduced in any form without written permission from the publisher. The Checkerboard Library™ is a trademark and logo of ABDO Publishing Company.

Printed in the United States.

Editor: John Hamilton
Graphic Design: Sue Hamilton
Cover Illustration: Neil Klinepier
Cover Photo: iStock Photo
Interior Photo Credits: AirPhoto/Jim Wark, AP Images, Comstock, Corbis, David Olson, Getty, Granger Collection, Harald Wehner, iStock Photo, L.L.Bean Inc. Archive Center, Library of Congress, Louis Norton, Maine Dept of Transportation, Maine Historical Society, Maine Secretary of State, Maine State Museum, Maine's First Ship, Milton Bradley/Hasbro, Mile High Maps, Mountain High Maps, North Wind Picture Archives, National Portrait Gallery, One Mile Up, Random House Publishing, Portland Schooner Company, Robert English, and the US Postal Service.
Statistics: State population statistics taken from 2008 U.S. Census Bureau estimates. City and town population statistics taken from July 1, 2007, U.S. Census Bureau estimates. Land and water area statistics taken from 2000 Census, U.S. Census Bureau.

Library of Congress Cataloging-in-Publication Data

Jensen, Niels R., 1949-
Maine / Niels Jensen.
p. cm. -- (The United States)
Includes index.
ISBN 978-1-60453-654-6
1. Maine--Juvenile literature. I. Title.

F19.3.J46 2010
974.1--dc22

2008051045

Table of Contents

Pine Tree State

Maine is the largest state in New England, and the first to see the morning light. It is famous for its rugged coastline, rolling mountains, and deep forests. In fact, it is named the Pine Tree State because of the large numbers of pine trees that cover the area.

Maine is a place where people come to enjoy the great outdoors. From Acadia National Park to Maine's charming coastal towns, the state's natural beauty is treasured.

Logging and shipbuilding in Maine began in the 1600s. These industries continue to this day. Maine is also one of the world's biggest producers of paper.

Bordered by the Atlantic Ocean, the state is well known for its fish and tasty lobster.

"Portland Head and its light seem to symbolize the state of Maine—rocky coast, breaking waves, sparkling water, and clear, pure salt air."
—Edward Rowe Snow, historian

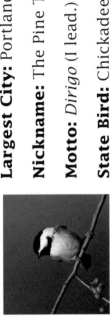

Quick Facts

Name: Some think Maine may be a sailing reference to the mainland. Others believe Maine was named in 1639 by England's King Charles I in honor of his queen, Henrietta Maria, who owned the province of Mayne in her homeland of France.

State Capital: Augusta, population 18,367

Date of Statehood: March 15, 1820 (23rd state)

Population: 1,316,456 (40th-most populous state)

Area (Total Land and Water): 35,385 square miles (91,647 sq km), 39th-largest state

Largest City: Portland, population 62,825

Nickname: The Pine Tree State

Motto: *Dirigo* (I lead.)

State Bird: Chickadee

White Pine Cone & Tassel

Mt. Katahdin

Atlantic Ocean

State Flower: White Pine Cone and Tassel

State Gem: Tourmaline

State Tree: White Pine Tree

State Song: "State of Maine Song"

Highest Point: Mt. Katahdin, 5,268 feet (1,606 m)

Lowest Point: Atlantic Ocean, 0 ft. (0 m)

Average July Temperature: 66°F (19°C)

Record High Temperature: 105°F (41°C), July 10, 1911, in North Bridgton

Average January Temperature: 14°F (-10°C)

Record Low Temperature: -48°F (-44°C), January 19, 1925, in Van Buren

Average Annual Precipitation: 43 inches (109 cm)

Number of U.S. Senators: 2

Number of U.S. Representatives: 2

U.S. Postal Service Abbreviation: ME

Geography

Maine is the most eastern state on the Atlantic Coast. There are nearly 5,100 streams and rivers, and 6,000 lakes and ponds. The coast is about 3,500 miles (5,600 km) long.

This area is part of the Appalachian Mountains. These mountains were created more than 400 million years ago when huge pieces of the earth's crust were pushed together. Mile-thick (1.6 km) glaciers grew and then melted across the area. Left behind were rocks, gravel, sand, and other materials. The melted water carved valleys and created lakes.

The rugged White Mountains in the western part of the state is an area of peaks, lakes, and woods. To the north are the Longfellow Mountains. Located here is Mt. Katahdin. At 5,268 feet (1,606 m), it is the state's highest point.

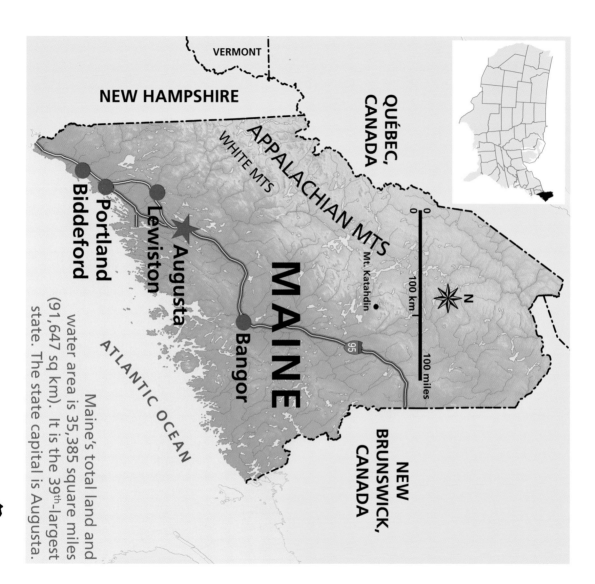

VERMONT

NEW HAMPSHIRE

QUÉBEC,
CANADA

APPALACHIAN MTS

WHITE MTS

Mt. Katahdin

MAINE

Biddeford

Portland

Lewiston

Augusta

Bangor

95

N

0
0
100 km
100 miles

ATLANTIC OCEAN

NEW
BRUNSWICK,
CANADA

Maine's total land and water area is 35,385 square miles (91,647 sq km). It is the 39th-largest state. The state capital is Augusta.

The Aroostook Plateau in northern Maine is filled with forested rolling hills, good farmland, and many streams and lakes. The area has many different types of wildlife.

The Uplands region in northern Maine is an area of rolling hills, good farmland, and many streams and lakes. The Aroostook Plateau is in the Uplands region.

The Coastal Lowlands have beautiful beaches, bays, creeks, marshes, and ponds. There are a lot of rocky cliffs and outcroppings. The region is an example of a "drowned coast." When the water from the melting glaciers made the sea rise, the ocean covered the coastal land. This changed hills into islands and valleys into bays. Some of Maine's more than 2,000 coastal islands are the tops of those hills.

Maine's coast is dotted with more than 2,000 islands.

Climate and Weather

A snowstorm in Lewiston, Maine.

Maine has a humid continental climate. That means it has warm, mild summers and cold winters. July's average temperature is 66° Fahrenheit (19°C). The average January temperature is 14° Fahrenheit (-10°C). Maine's winters are warmer than other northern states that are farther inland.

The ocean affects the state's climate. It also causes the weather to change quickly. It can go from bright and sunny to windy and stormy within an hour.

The state's northern half gets the most snow and coldest temperatures. Blizzards sometimes strike the state. Maine's coastal areas have more moderate conditions.

12

Severe storms occasionally hit Maine. Some of them are hurricanes. Usually these violent storms have traveled up the East Coast, weakening as they go. However, they are still very dangerous and destructive. Winds over 81 miles per hour (130 kph) have been reported.

Waves crash off Five Islands, Maine. High winds and rough seas sometimes keep lobster boats in their harbors.

Plants and Animals

Maine's Governor John Baldacci taps a maple tree in 2007.

Vast forests cover about 90 percent of Maine. Ash, beech, birch, elm, maple, oak, pine, spruce, hemlock, and willow trees all grow in the state. The official state tree is the white pine. The state flower is the white pine cone and tassel. Maple trees turn out about 300,000 gallons (1.1 million liters) of syrup every year. Maine is the second-largest producer of maple syrup in the United States.

With all the trees come many different bird populations. There are cardinals, cormorants, cranes, ducks, eagles, falcons, larks, loons, geese, gulls, herons, sandpipers, terns, vultures, warblers, wrens, and more. The state bird is the chickadee.

Puffin with Fish

Great Blue Heron

Herring Gull

Maine has a healthy animal population. There are beaver, black bear, bobcat, coyote, deer, fisher, fox, lynx, marten, mink, muskrat, rabbit, raccoon, snowshoe hare, woodchuck, and many others. Moose is the state animal of Maine.

The state's waters are famous for fishing. Its rivers and lakes have bass, trout, pike, perch, landlocked salmon, muskellunge, sunfish, and many other fish. In the Atlantic Ocean, fishermen love to catch mackerel, striped bass, bluefish, and the powerful bluefin tuna. Shellfish include clams, crabs, and oysters. Maine is famous for its lobsters.

The Gulf of Maine has finback, humpback, minke and pilot whales, as well as dolphins, orcas, porpoises, seals, and sea turtles. There are whale-watching cruises available along the coasts.

Lobster

Lynx

Deer

Moose is the state animal of Maine.

History

Native Americans came to the Maine area soon after the glaciers melted, about 10,000 years ago. The Red Paint People lived along Maine's coast about 4,000 years ago. They left tools and red paint in their graves. Maine's Algonquian tribes hunted, fished, grew crops, and lived in villages.

In 1604, the French started the first European settlement on an island in the St. Croix River. It failed. Englishman George Popham built a settlement at the Kennebec River in 1607. It was abandoned after a year. Some of the colonists sailed back on a large ship named *Virginia of Sagadahoc*. It may have been the first European ship built in America.

A model of the *Virginia*.

French missionaries come ashore in Somes Sound, Mount Desert Island, Maine. The French started the first European colony in Maine in 1604.

The French kept trying to get a foothold in the area. In 1613, the English destroyed a Jesuit mission on Mount Desert Island. The border between the French and English territories remained unclear for a long time.

In 1622, the English Council for New England gave the area between the Kennebec and Merrimack Rivers to Sir Ferdinando Gorges and John Mason. They split the land in 1629. Gorges got the land east of the Piscataqua River. It became the province of Maine.

Settlers soon arrived. They were mainly loggers, traders, and fishermen. After Gorges died in 1647, Massachusetts gained control of the colony. His family finally sold their rights in 1677. Maine became a separate district of Massachusetts.

Early Maine settlers drying and salting fish on the shore.

King Philip's War in 1675 brought fighting to Maine. The city of Portland was burned. A long series of hard-fought French and Indian wars followed until the 1763 Treaty of Paris. It gave all of the French areas east of the Mississippi River to the British.

Great Britain wanted to tax its American colonies to pay for the wars. However, the British leaders would not allow Americans to be represented in government. The people of Maine fought against the new taxes. A mob seized tax stamps in Portland in 1765. Colonists in York, Maine, burned a shipment of tea in 1774. The following year, the Revolutionary War began.

English explorers sailing up the Penobscot River.

The Revolutionary War ended in 1783. At that time, Maine and Massachusetts were one state. However, in the years ahead, Massachusetts officials seemed more worried about their own area's defense than Maine's. The people of Maine decided to take action. Maine became the 23rd state on March 15, 1820. It entered the Union as a free state as part of the Missouri Compromise.

In 1839, a problem arose over the border between Maine and New Brunswick, Canada, which was then a colony of Great Britain. Maine and Great Britain nearly went to war. The dispute was settled with the signing of the Webster-Ashburton Treaty of 1842.

There was a strong anti-slavery movement in Maine before the Civil War (1861-1865). About 75,000 Mainers joined the Union army. Some fought at major battles, such as Gettysburg and Bull Run.

After the war, the clothing, paper, and leather industries grew. Fishing and shipbuilding continued to be important businesses. By the 1890s, some rivers were used to generate electricity.

In the 1900s, clothing mills declined, while paper and pulp production increased. There were fewer family farms. Some fields again became forest. Because of the beauty of the area, Maine's tourism grew into big business.

Lobster fishing on the Grand Manan Channel in 1894.

Did You Know?

- Eastport, Maine, is the first city in the United States to get the morning light.

- There are about 60 lighthouses along Maine's coastline. The original Portland Head Light was first lit in 1791, when George Washington was president.

- The Bush family has a vacation home in Kennebunkport, Maine. Former Presidents George H.W. Bush and George W. Bush are often seen there. Known as Walker's Point, the beautiful home has hosted many important politicians and visitors from around the world.

- The "Maine Coon" is a large cat that is native to the state. Tales were once told to visitors that the cat was a cross between a regular cat and a raccoon. Really it is just a very strong and healthy cat breed that over 300 years developed a long fur coat to survive Maine's harsh weather. The Maine Coon is one of the oldest natural cat breeds in North America.

- In 1972, the Penobscot and Passamaquoddy tribes filed suit against the federal government for the northern two-thirds of Maine. They claimed Congress never ratified a 1794 treaty. The United States settled the suit by paying them $81.5 million.

People

After a hunting trip that left him with cold, wet feet, **Leon Leonwood Bean** (1872–1967) designed a boot with leather tops and rubber bottoms. This was the start of his business. Today L.L.Bean has since grown into a major catalog and retail company featuring sports and outdoor clothing and equipment. Bean was born in Greenwood, Maine.

Stephen King (1947-) is an author, actor, columnist, screenwriter, director, and producer. He is famous for his popular, terror-filled stories, such as *Carrie* and *Salem's Lot*. King is known as the King of Horror. He is from Portland, Maine.

Milton Bradley (1836-1911) was a printer who developed many famous board games. His first was called *The Checkered Game of Life*, which came out in 1860. Today, his company's other famous games include *Battleship*, *Candy Land*, and *Operation*. Bradley also invented a one-armed paper cutter. He was born in Vienna, Maine.

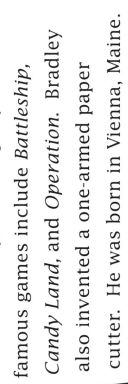

Dorothea Dix (1802-1887) pioneered the care and treatment of the mentally ill. She was also the Union army's superintendent of nurses during the Civil War. She was from Hampden, Maine.

Henry Wadsworth Longfellow (1807-1882)

was one of the most popular and successful poets of his time. His poems are still widely read. His best-known works include *The Song of Hiawatha*, *Paul Revere's Ride*, and *Evangeline*. Longfellow was born in Portland, Maine.

Nelson A. Rockefeller (1908-1979)

was vice president of the United States under President Gerald Ford from 1974 to 1977. Before that, he was the governor of New York from 1959 to 1973. He was also involved with charity work. He was born in Bar Harbor, Maine.

Cities

Augusta was chosen as Maine's capital in 1827. It was located between several of the state's main cities. It is by the Kennebec River, which once provided waterpower for many sawmills and factories. Today, the city's economy is dependent on government services and colleges. The University of Maine at Augusta has about 6,000 students.

The city's population is 18,367.

Maine's capital has been in Augusta since 1827.

Portland is Maine's largest city with a population of 62,825. It was the state's capital from 1820-1827. The city was destroyed by fire four times, but has always been rebuilt. Today, it is an important cultural and business center with banks, colleges, hospitals, restaurants, and shops. Portland's harbor is one of the busiest in New England. Tourists enjoy visiting the city and Portland Harbor.

Lewiston is the state's second-largest city with a population of 35,234. It is located right next to **Auburn**, whose population is 23,203. Together, they are referred to as the Twin Cities. Beverages, car parts, countertops, fabrics, food products, metal, paper, shoes, and many other products are made in the area. There are also distribution and phone centers. The health care industry is the largest employer.

The Androscoggin River separates the cities of Lewiston and Auburn.

32

Bangor, Maine, is built next to the Penobscot River. The city burned down in the Great Fire of 1911. It was rebuilt using many of the best materials and building designs of the time. Today, it is still a beautiful city.

Bangor serves as a commercial center for the central, eastern, and northern parts of the state. The population is 31,853. The city was once home to shipyards and sawmills, but the wood-related industry switched to paper and pulp production in the 1900s. The city has banks, colleges, shops, and government services.

Transportation

Maine's largest commercial airport is Portland International Jetport. It handles more than 1.5 million passengers per year. Other commercial airports are at Augusta, Bangor, Bar Harbor, Presque Isle, and Rockland.

The Portland International Jetport.

About 375,000 passengers ride Amtrak's Downeaster train, which runs from Portland, Maine, to Boston, Massachusetts. There are six railways hauling freight on about 1,100 miles (1,770 km) of track. Some railroads go to Canada.

Amtrak's Downeaster Train

34

The state has about 21,000 miles (33,796 km) of roads and 2,700 bridges. The main interstate highway is I-95.

The Port of Portland is an ocean gateway. More than 25 million tons (23 million metric tons) of freight pass through it every year. The large cruise liners use the harbor, serving around 50,000 passengers. Each year, ferries move about 900,000 passengers and 40,000 cars to other cities and islands in the area.

Ferries move passengers and cars to other cities and islands in the area.

Natural Resources

Maine has 17 million acres (7 million ha) of forest. It is one of the largest producers of paper. There are loggers, sawmills, energy firms, and equipment makers. Maine's forests are also used in the sports and tourism industries. In all, wood-related businesses bring in $6.2 billion to the state's economy.

Logs are loaded onto a truck at a Maine paper mill.

Maine has about 7,100 farms, with an average size of 190 acres (77 ha). Farms bring in a total income of $1.2 billion. Potatoes, dairy products, and eggs are among the state's major products.

The traditional way to harvest Maine blueberries is by using a rake (shown at the lower right).

The state is the largest grower of wild blueberries in the world. Some of the farms supply naturally organic fruits, vegetables, and meat.

The commercial fishing catch is valued at about $375 million. Maine lobster is especially famous, and accounts for nearly 80 percent of the fishing income. Local fish farms also produce oysters, mussels, and salmon.

A lobsterman holds two of his catch.

Industry

Maine is a wonderful vacationland. People come to see its many scenic lighthouses, cruise its coastline, and hike its woods. Tourism is a $10 billion business.

Since forests cover most of the state, it is no surprise that paper and wood products are one of Maine's most important businesses.

Maine also makes computer components, electronic products, leather, shoes, and fabric. Fairchild Semiconductor has its headquarters here. Other high technology companies include General Dynamics and Pratt & Whitney. The Jackson Laboratory works with genetics and biomedical research.

The *Bagheera* brings visitors to see the Portland Head Light. The ship was built in East Boothbay, Maine, more than 80 years ago.

The state is home to L.L.Bean. This catalog and retail company sells sports clothing and equipment.

Maine has an active boat and shipbuilding industry. Located on New Hampshire's border, the Portsmouth Naval Shipyard services the nation's nuclear-powered submarines.

In October 2008, the USS *New Hampshire* submarine is ready for active duty at the Portsmouth Naval Shipyard.

Sports

Maine is a wonderful place to enjoy the great outdoors. There are wilderness areas, tall mountains, rivers, and a beautiful coastline.

The northernmost start of the famous Appalachian Trail begins at Maine's Mt. Katahdin. Hikers can take the trail south through the center of the state, or visit hiking trails at Acadia National Park or more than 30 state parks.

A hiker in Acadia National Park.

An ocean kayaker near Ogunquit Beach, Maine.

The state has camping, biking, golfing, horseback riding, rock climbing, and skydiving. Hunting is a long-standing tradition.

There are also many water-related activities. People enjoy canoeing, boating, fishing, kayaking, sailing, scuba diving, swimming, and whitewater rafting. The beaches are beautiful.

There are a large number of great ski, snowboarding, and cross-country skiing areas. Other winter sports include dog sledding, ice fishing, ice skating, snowmobiling and snowshoeing.

A backcountry skier pauses to view Mt. Katahdin from Katahdin Lake in Maine's Baxter State Park.

Entertainment

Maine hosts many festivals and fairs, celebrating foods, cultures, the arts, music, and more. The Great Falls Balloon Festival is a charity event that is held in the summer in the Lewiston-Auburn area. It began in 1992, and now attracts more than 25 balloon racers and 100,000 festivalgoers.

A hot air balloon floats gently over Auburn, Maine, during the Great Falls Balloon Festival.

Professional and community theater groups perform plays throughout Maine. There are two professional ballet companies.

Bangor and Portland both have professional symphony orchestras. There are also opera companies and other classical music groups. The state has a tradition of ethnic and folk music, and there are country, blues, jazz, and other popular music performances.

The Maine State Aquarium is located at West Boothbay Harbor, Maine. It features a monster-sized 23-pound (10-kg) lobster. The state's largest amusement park and zoo is at York.

Sailboat races are popular. Maine has several horse and auto racing tracks.

Teens race against other boats as part of their sailing school training.

Timeline

2000 BC—The Red Paint People and other Native Americans arrive in the area.

1629—Sir Ferdinando Gorges is given the land east of the Piscataqua River. This becomes the province of Maine.

1783—The Revolutionary War ends with America gaining its freedom from Great Britain. Maine and Massachusetts are one state at this time.

1820—Maine becomes the 23rd state on March 15, 1820. Portland is named as the capital.

1827—Augusta becomes the state capital.

Daniel Webster

Lord Ashburton

1842—The signing of the Webster-Ashburton Treaty ends a border dispute between Maine and New Brunswick, Canada.

1861—The Civil War begins. Maine stays in the Union, sending 75,000 troops to fight.

1900s—Maine's logging, shipbuilding, and fishing industries increase.

1980—The U.S. government pays the Penobscot and Passamaquoddy tribes for the northern two-thirds of Maine.

2008—A terrible ice storm leaves millions in Maine without power for several days.

Glossary

Colony—A colony is the establishment of a settlement in a new location. It is often ruled by another country.

Glaciers—Huge sheets of ice that grow and shrink as the climate changes. They shape the land beneath them.

Hurricane—A violent wind storm that begins in tropical ocean waters. Hurricanes cause dangerously high tides and bring deadly waves, driving rain, and even tornados. Hurricanes break up and die down after reaching land.

Mission—A religious settlement or outpost, which usually has a church and a school.

Missouri Compromise—An agreement created in 1820 that said that Missouri could be a slave state, but the territories north and west of Missouri could not have slavery. To keep a balance in Congress, Missouri was admitted to the Union as a slave state, and Maine as a free state.

New England—An area in the northeast United States, consisting of the states of Maine, Vermont, New Hampshire, Massachusetts, Rhode Island, and Connecticut.

Revolutionary War—The war fought between the American colonies and Great Britain from 1775-1783. It is also known as the War of Independence or the American Revolution.

Tax Stamps—An actual stamp that was placed on items or documents to prove that a government tax had been paid.

Webster-Ashburton Treaty—An agreement establishing the border between Maine and New Brunswick, Canada. The treaty also established other United States and Canada boundaries. It allowed the U.S. to use the St. John River, and called for the two countries to work together to stop the slave trade on the African coast. The treaty was created in 1842 by Daniel Webster of the United States and Lord Ashburton of Great Britain. At the time, Great Britain ruled Canada. The treaty ended the possibility of fighting between the countries.

Index